© 1990 Franklin Watts

First published in Great Britain
   1990 by
Franklin Watts
96 Leonard Street
London EC2A 4RH

First published in the USA by
Franklin Watts Inc
387 Park Avenue South
New York
NY 10016

First published in Australia by
Franklin Watts
14 Mars Road
Lane Cove
NSW 2066

UK ISBN: 0 7496 0059 4

Printed in Belgium

Series Editor
Norman Barrett

Designed by
K and Co

Photographs by
Agusta
Bell Helicopters
Boeing Vertol Company
Hughes Helicopters
NATO
Royal Navy
US Department of Defense
US Navy
US Navy/PHCS R. W. Bayles
US Navy/PHCM C. Pedrick
Westland Helicopters

Technical Consultant
Bernie Fitzsimons

The Picture World of

Military Helicopters

R. J. Stephen

CONTENTS

Franklin Watts

London • New York • Sydney • Toronto

Introduction

Helicopters have several roles in modern warfare. They are used in battlefields on land and at sea.

Armed with weapons, military helicopters are a powerful attacking force on land. Assault helicopters carry men to the battlefields and have enough firepower to support them.

At sea, helicopters are used for such duties as search and rescue and anti-submarine warfare.

▽ A Lynx gives a demonstration of rapid rocket fire. Attack helicopters provide firepower against light armour and infantry.

△ A formation of SH-3 Sea King anti-submarine helicopters of the US Navy.

▷ A CH-47 Chinook with a heavy shipment of supplies suspended underneath its body. These powerful twin-rotor helicopters are used to carry troops, weapons and other equipment into battle.

General duties

Some kinds of military helicopters are designed for special duties, such as attack or transport. Others are equipped to handle more than one kind of task. These are called utility or general-purpose helicopters.

General-purpose helicopters may be used for reconnaissance and light transport of troops and supplies. They are often armed, so that they can defend themselves. They may even carry missiles.

△ The Battlefield Lynx as an assault helicopter, carrying troops and arms to the battlefield.

△ In its anti-tank role, the Battlefield Lynx has formidable firepower. Up to eight guided weapons can be fired singly or in rapid succession, and the cabin holds another eight missile reload rounds.

▷ The Battlefield Lynx in its support role, evacuating casualties.

Gunships

All armed helicopters can be used for attacking the enemy. But some, the gunships or attack helicopters, are designed purely for attack.

Gunships hunt and destroy enemy tanks and helicopters. They carry an array of weapons and missiles. High speed and heavy armour plating underneath help to protect them against attack from the ground.

▽ An AH-1S HueyCobra firing rockets. Gunships have a crew of two, the gunner seated in front with the pilot behind him. The HueyCobra was the first anti-tank attack helicopter and is the chief gunship of the US Army.

◁ A 530MG Defender in camouflage colours. Despite its name, the Defender is an attack helicopter, and like most gunships packs an enormous amount of firepower for its size.

▽ A-129 Mangustas show the sleek lines of a typical gunship. Gunships are designed to present as small a target as possible to the enemy.

◁ A heavily armed AH-1W SuperCobra. Rockets are carried in pods of 19 at each side. Outside these are anti-tank missiles with homing devices.

△ A SuperCobra firing a Sidewinder air-to-air missile. This deadly rocket-powered missile homes in on the infra-red heat waves of an enemy aircraft.

◁ The engines of the AH-64 Apache are heavily shrouded. This is to protect it from shoulder-launched heat-seeking missiles that might be fired at it from the battlefield.

Assault and lift

Assault helicopters lift troops and equipment to the battlefield. They often have to support them until other supply routes are established.
   These tasks may be carried out by utility helicopters or by medium- or heavy-lift helicopters, depending on an army's requirements.

△ The Westland Lynx is an all-round assault helicopter, well-armed and capable of carrying nine combat troops.

▷ The CH-47 Chinook is used for heavy-lift duties behind the battlefield.

◁ The Sikorsky Skycrane is a heavy-lift helicopter designed to carry heavy items either suspended underneath, as here, or fixed under its slim body.

△ The medium-lift Westland WS 70A shows its ability to lift heavy equipment while carrying a range of rockets and other armaments.

◁ A squadron of WS 70A's disgorge troops straight into action. The WS 70A is based closely on the Sikorsky Black Hawk.

Naval helicopters

Helicopters are as much a part of naval warfare as the ships that carry them. They are used in various attacking roles and perform general duties such as supply, transport and search and rescue.

Naval helicopters, equipped with special detection methods use torpedoes to attack submarines. Some carry long-range missiles for use against large warships.

▽ A small platform at the stern of a ship is all a helicopter needs for taking off and landing. But it calls for skilful handling to land a helicopter when the ship is rolling in rough seas.

◁ A Lynx dipping sonar. Sonar is a sound system for locating submerged submarines.

▽ Naval submarines land men and equipment from supply ships. Helicopters play an important part when invasion forces are trying to establish themselves on shore.

△ A view through a helicopter's rotor blades of crewmen carrying out maintenance on a Sea Stallion.

◁ A Navy Lynx armed with missiles flies off from the storm-tossed HMS *Minerva*. The Lynx is used to detect and attack both submarines and surface vessels.

▷ Sea Cobras (front) and Sea Knights packed onto the forward flight deck of an assault ship.

△ An SH-3 Sea King
picks up a Firebee, a
pilotless aircraft used
for target practice.

▷ The Boeing Vertol
CH-46 Sea Knight is
used for assault work,
search and rescue
missions, transport
and vertrep (vertical
replenishment), as
here.

△ The SH-60B
Seahawk operates
mainly from destroyers
and frigates in anti-
submarine and anti-
ship missions.

▷ The Soviet Kamov
Ka-25 "Hormone" is
an anti-submarine
helicopter.

Research is constantly being carried out to improve the design of helicopters, particularly in the United States, Europe and the Soviet Union.

Stronger materials and fresh ideas make the development of the helicopter one of the most exciting stories in the progress of aviation.

△ The EH 101 is a joint British-Italian project. Built with the latest lightweight materials, the EH 101 will have speed, considerable lifting power and unequalled safety features. The same basic airframe is designed to produce aircraft for naval, utility and civil use.

The V-22 Osprey, an American development, is a tilt-rotor craft. Its rotors, used for taking off, landing and hovering, tilt forward to serve as propellers for fast forward flight.

▷ An artist's impression of V-22s in action.

▽ The V-22 dipping sonar in its possible naval role in anti-submarine warfare.

Facts

H for "helicopter"

The chief Soviet military helicopters are Kamovs and Mils. They are known in the West by code names, all beginning with the letter H, such as Hare, Hind and Havoc.

△ The Mi-24 "Hind" gunship.

In-flight refuelling

There are some situations where it is difficult or inconvenient for a helicopter to land. In such cases, refuelling in mid-air becomes necessary.

Apart from minor experiments in the air and with ground vehicles, the first successful in-flight refuelling was carried out during the Vietnam war, when rescue helicopters needed to remain on patrol for long periods. The standard tanker aircraft could not fly at speeds slow enough to refuel helicopters, so the Hercules was modified for this purpose.

But it was not until 1985 that the first in-flight refuelling of the heavy transport Chinook took place. Again, it was behind a Hercules flying tanker.

△ The first in-flight refuelling of a Chinook takes place in August 1985 over Pennsylvania. A US Army CH-47D Chinook hooks up behind an Air Force HC-130 Hercules, inserting an 11.5-metre (38-ft) fuel probe into the tanker's 23-metre (76-ft) fuel line.

Tilt-rotor craft

The development of tilt-rotor aircraft has been going on for

26

more than 30 years. The V-22 Osprey was part of a major US programme to produce a craft whose chief duty would be to carry marines into battle.

A total of over 600 V-22s was planned. But in 1989 the programme was threatened by heavy US government cuts in defence spending, though development continued.

△ The first flight of the V-22 tilt-rotor craft at Arlington, Texas, in March 1989.

Helicopters in Vietnam

The helicopter owes its development as a fighting machine to the war in Vietnam in the 1960s. The US Army used helicopters in its efforts to locate the guerrilla forces of the Vietcong.

Their chief small transport helicopter in Vietnam was the Bell UH-1 Iroquois, known as the Huey. Armed at first for self-protection, the Huey was developed as a gunship, with machine-guns, rockets and grenades.

As the war progressed, a new helicopter was designed, the AH-1 HueyCobra. AH-1s were narrower than the Huey and easier to camouflage on the ground. They were used for close support and attack roles.

Other helicopters that served in Vietnam included heavy transport machines such as the Chinook and reconnaissance craft such as the Bell OH-58A Kiowa.

△ A Huey in action in Vietnam.

Glossary

Assault helicopter
A helicopter that carries troops, arms and equipment to the battlefield.

Attack helicopter
A heavily armed helicopter designed solely for attacking the enemy. Attack helicopters are also called gunships.

Gunship
An attack helicopter.

Homing device
A device used to guide a missile to its target. Various kinds of homing devices are used. Some, such as that on the Sidewinder, home in on the hot exhausts of enemy aircraft. Others may be guided by optical means or by the operator sending adjustments to the missile's flight path along a wire.

Hovering
Hanging in the air without moving in any direction.

Reconnaissance
Seeking information, usually about enemy forces and their whereabouts.

Rotor
The spinning wings of a helicopter. A rotor may have up to eight separate blades.

Search and rescue
An operation, carried out on land or at sea, to locate men in trouble or cut off by the enemy and bring them back to base.

Sonar
A system for locating enemy submarines under water. It works by sending out sound waves and listening for their echo.

Tilt-rotor craft
An aircraft with rotors that can be tilted to serve as propellers in level flight.

Utility helicopter
A helicopter designed to carry out more than one kind of duty.

Index